Heaven

Songs for the Soul-Winning Church

Arranged by

Mike Speck

& Cliff Duren

Orchestrated by Wayne Haun

Contents

MIKE SPECK
MUSIC

lillenas
PUBLISHING COMPANY

lillenas.com

I'm Still Standing

with
Standing on the Promises
Trust in the Lord

Words and Music by
KURT CARR
Arr. by Mike Speck
and Cliff Duren

on___ the Word_____ that's in___ my heart.___

CD: 2
CD: 47

—___ Oh!_____

G♭ B♭m7 C♭M7   D♭   E♭m7   F♭   C♭   F♭   C♭/D♭

I'm___ still stand   -   ing,___   I'm___ still trust-

D♭/E♭   Cm7 D♭M7   D♭2/F E♭2/G A♭

*"Standing on the Promises"

SOLO

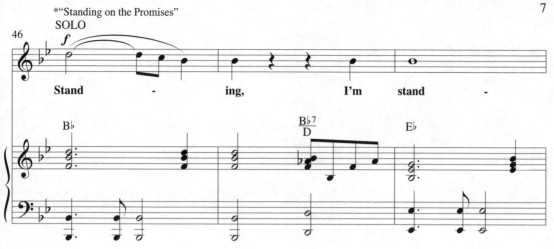

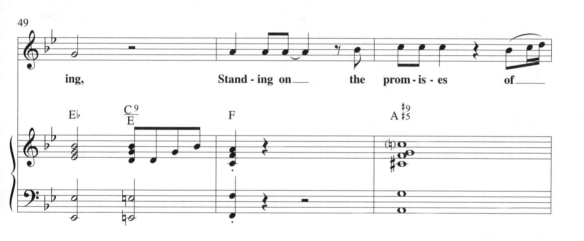

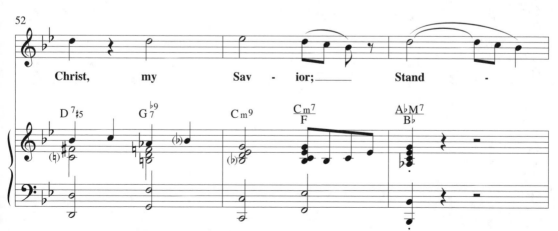

New Day Dawning

with
We'll Soon Be Done with Troubles and Trials
When I Get Carried Away

Words and Music by
JOEL LINDSEY
Arr. by Mike Speck
and Cliff Duren

16

brand new morn - ing. Pack - in' my bags for a heav - en - ly jour - ney.

I can't wait__ to be__ there.   I can't wait__ to be__

14

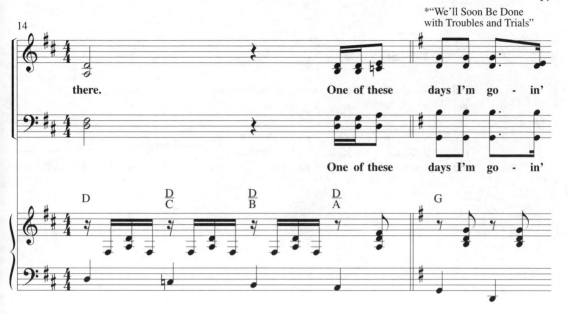

there.   One of these   days I'm go - in'

One of these   days I'm go - in'

D   D/C   D/B   D/A   G

home   where   no   sor - rows   ev - er come.

home   where   no   sor - rows   ev - er come. We'll   soon____   be

G

Page 19

CD: 10
CD: 55

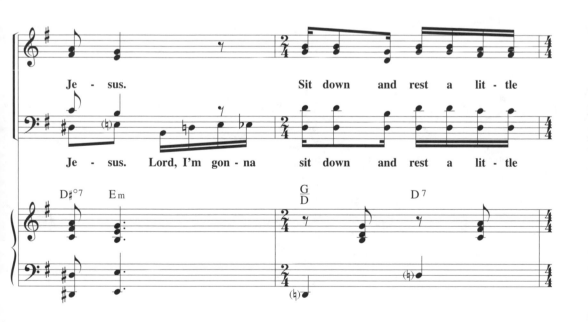

CD: 10
CD: 55
20
all that glo - ry share. Sit down be-side of my
all that glo - ry share. And I'm gon-na sit down be-side of my
C
G/D
Je - sus. Sit down and rest a lit - tle
Je - sus. Lord, I'm gon - na sit down and rest a lit - tle
D♯°7
E m
G/D
D 7

*"When I Get Carried Away"

I'm gon-na let the glo - ry roll___ when the roll is called___ in glo - ry. I'm gon-na get be - side of my-self when I get be-side___ the King that___ day. I'm gon-na have the

26

Only One Way

Words and Music by
MIKE SPECK and
REBECCA J. PECK
*Arr. by Mike Speck
and Cliff Duren*

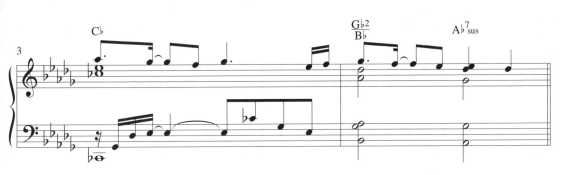

Ev - 'ry hu-man heart feels the long-ing; A

in Je - sus as Sav - ior.

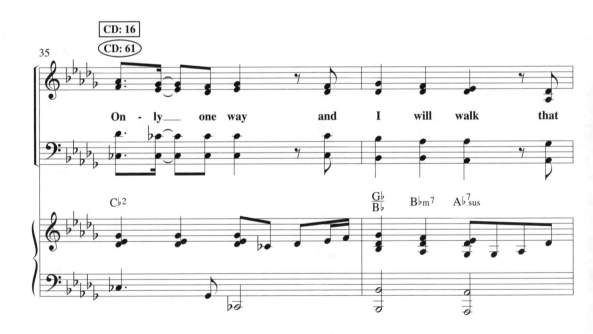

CD: 16
CD: 61

On - ly___ one way and I will walk that

SOLO *more energy*

Down the nar-row road_ to Cal - v'ry,

way.

Oo,

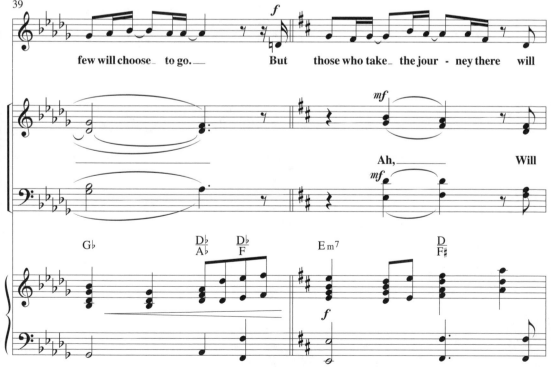

few will choose_ to go. _ But those who take_ the jour - ney there will

Ah, _ Will

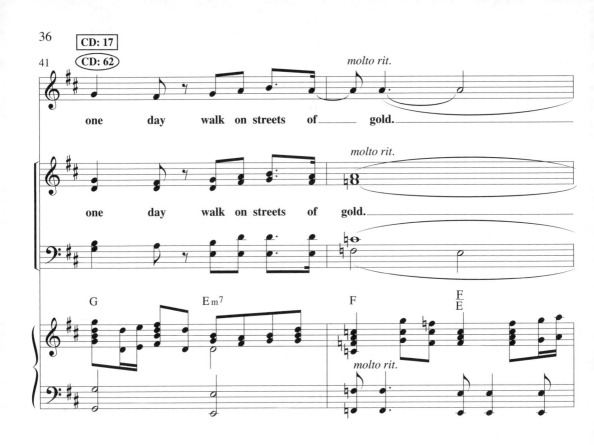

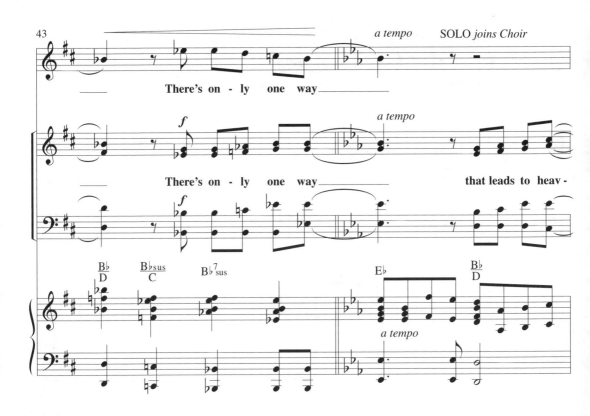

CD: 18
CD: 63

View the City

with
Since Jesus Came into My Heart
I'll Fly Away
Looking for a City

Words and Music by
AY'RON LEWIS,
ADRIANN LEWIS
and AUNDREA LEWIS
*Arr. by Mike Speck
and Cliff Duren*

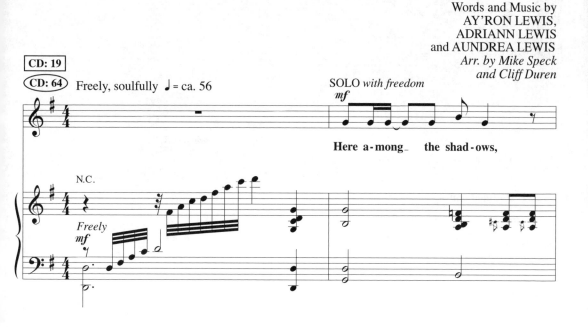

42

I'm gon-na view that ho - ly cit - y one__ of these days.

SOLO *ad libs and/or joins Choir throughout*

44

31 *"Since Jesus Came into My Heart"

go there— to dwell in— that cit - y— I know.

G7

33

And I'm

I'm gon-na view that ho - ly cit - y one— of these days. Hal-le-lu - jah!

C7

G

48

hap - py,— so hap - py— as on - ward— I go.

View that ho - ly cit - y one of these days.

*"I'll Fly Away"

39

Some glad morn - ing when this life is o'er,____

A♭

41

I'm gon-na view that ho - ly cit - y one__ of these days. Hal-le-lu - jah!

D♭7

A♭

Go - in' to my home on God's ce - les - tial shore.

View that ho - ly cit - y one of these days.

47

I'll   fly a - way, O glo - ry. I'll   fly a -

A♭   D♭

50

way,   hal-le-lu-jah! I'm   gon-na view that ho - ly

A♭

CD: 23
CD: 68

52

cit - y,   view that ho - ly cit - y   one of these

A♭ $\frac{A♭9}{C}$ D♭   D°7 $\frac{A♭}{E♭}$ $F7^{♭9}$ B♭9 $\frac{B♭m7}{E♭}$

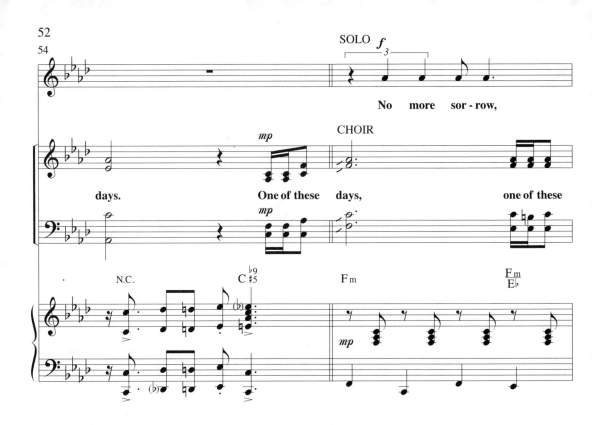

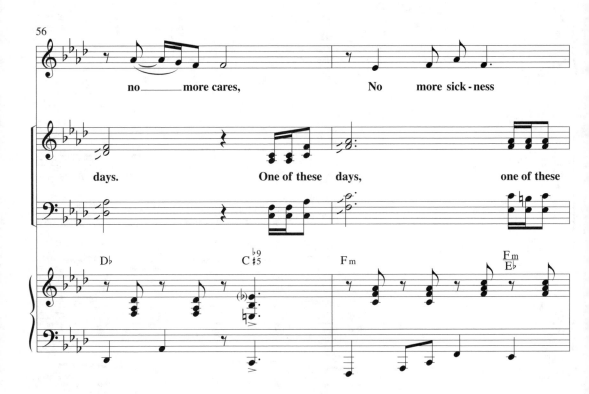

54

*"Looking for a City"

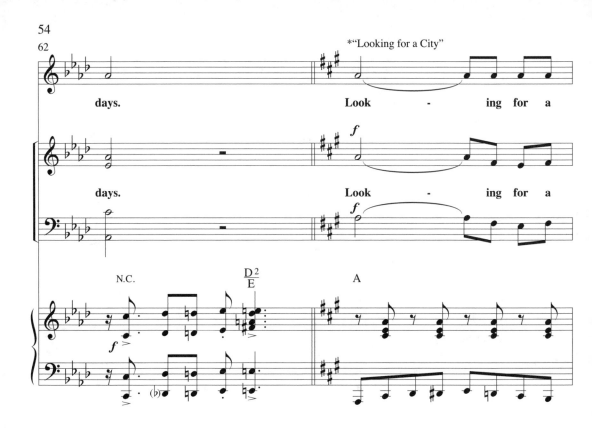

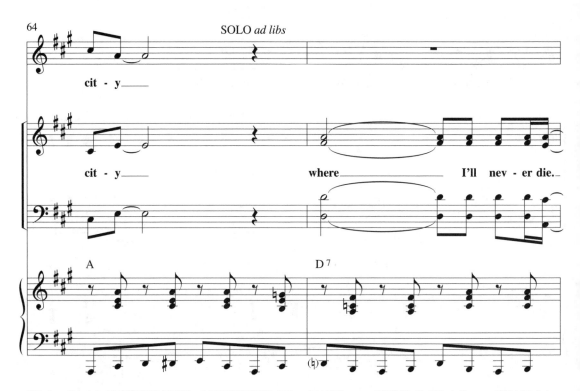

I'm gon-na view that ho - ly cit - y one__ of these days. Hal-le-lu - jah!

(to pg. 56, meas. 75)

(to pg. 56, meas. 75)

days.

(8) SOLO *ad libs*

Soon We Will See

with

What a Day That Will Be
Touring That City
That Will Be Glory for Me

Words and Music by
RODNEY GRIFFIN
*Arr. by Mike Speck
and Cliff Duren*

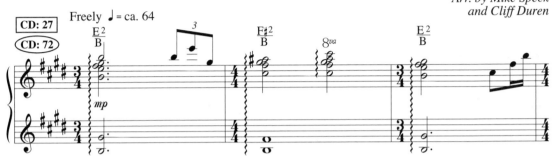

day ... when no heart - aches shall

come. ... No more clouds in the

sky, no more tears to dim these eyes.___

16

All is peace for - ev-er - more on that

19

hap - py gold - en shore. What a day, what a

CD: 28

CD: 73

22 Faster, in two ♩. = ca. 42

day!

CHOIR

Soon we will see the por - tals of glo - ry;

Soon we will see the Great I AM;

Soon we will hear the an - gels cry ho - ly;

CD: 29
30 CD: 74

Soon we will see_____ the Lamb.

C   F
           C   F   C

32

Soon we will see   the por - tals   of glo - ry;

F

34

Soon we will see   the Great___ I   AM;___

C   F   C$^7_{sus}$

find me there on the streets____ so pret-ty, Made of

gold so pure and so bright. With

Je - sus, the One____ who gave me the vic - t'ry, Who____

CD: 31
CD: 76

*"That Will Be Glory for Me"

Worship at the Throne

includes
Agnus Dei
Worthy Is the Lamb
O Come, Let Us Adore Him
I Bowed on My Knees and Cried, "Holy!"

Arr. by Mike Speck
and Cliff Duren

PLEASE NOTE: Copying of this product is NOT covered by CCLI licenses. For CCLI information call 1-800-234-2446.

74

84

The First Day of Forever

with

I'll Meet You in the Morning

Words and Music by
MARTY FUNDERBURK
and DONNA M. BEAUVAIS
*Arr. by Mike Speck
and Cliff Duren*

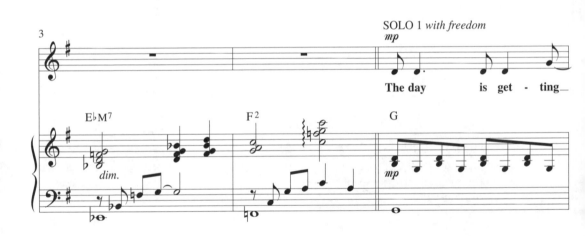

feel it in my___ spir-it, I'll___ soon be___ leav - ing

here. And in my mind___ I've___ gone there_____ a

thou - sand times or more. O how I just i -

88

with the One who died____ for me.____

Un - end - ing day of glad - ness

like I've nev - er known____ be - fore.____

The first day of for - ev - er will

last for - ev - er - more.

SOLO 2 *with freedom*

CD: 42
CD: 87

I

know   I'll see   my loved ones,   yes, we'll   gath - er o - ver_

there.   But there   is no   re - un - ion   that could

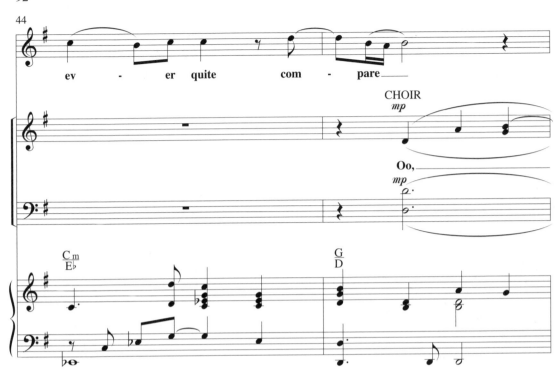

ev - er quite com - pare

CHOIR
mp

Oo,

mp

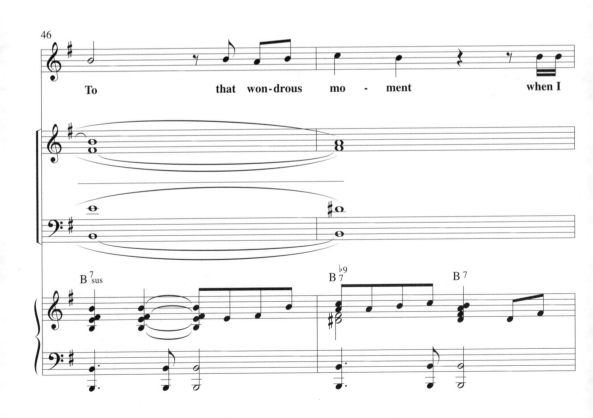

To that won-drous mo - ment when I

93

94

SOLO 3 *(Tenor or Alto)* *"I'll Meet You in the Morning"*

I'll meet you in the morn-ing

with a "how do you do?"

And we'll sit down by the riv-er

Optional Narration
(Running Time - Approximately 15 minutes)

I'm Still Standing

(Narration begins after I'm Still Standing *ends)*

WORSHIP LEADER: I'm still standing, holding and trusting in the truth that is contained in the blessed book we call the Bible. Why? Because I believe it is more than just a good book . . . it is God's actual words, penned as God Himself dictated them, to His prophets. It is God's letter to mankind, explaining the mysteries of life. It is a perfect record of all that has transpired and all that will transpire from the beginning of creation, to the end of the age.

It has withstood the test of time and will continue to endure the scrutiny of the skeptics and scoffers. Thousands of years old, it has never been proven wrong . . . not even once. It is truth without error . . . and I'm still standing on the promises that are revealed in its pages.

The Bible is why I believe there is a Heaven. Yet, if I had never seen or heard of the Bible, I would still believe there is something more to life than this present world. It could be that God has written it into the consciousness of every human . . . for nearly every culture on planet earth expresses awareness of an afterlife– every people group, both religious and pagan. From Aborigines, Polynesians and Native Americans to ancient Babylonians, Egyptians and Romans; there has always been the common thread that this present earth is not all there is.

One thing is for certain; all of us face the same inevitable moment, when we will take one final breath. The wealthy, the poor . . . the educated and uneducated . . . the simple and the sophisticated will all experience death. Three people die every second, 180 every minute; nearly 11,000 every hour. 250,000 people go[1] into eternity each and every day.

According to scripture, there are only two places a person can spend eternity . . . either in Heaven, where there is unending peace and joy, or Hell, where there is everlasting suffering. I have made preparations and reservations for Heaven. I've double checked them. I have absolutely no doubt *(music begins)* that I am already counted as a citizen of Heaven.

New Day Dawning

(Narration begins after New Day Dawning *ends)*

WORSHIP LEADER: Some people spend more time planning and preparing for a vacation than they do for their eternal destination.[2] God's Word teaches that Heaven is a real, physical place. It is a place where all of the bad has been taken away and contentment and wonder never ends. Hell is just as real . . . a place that no one but the foolish or ignorant would want to go.

What does it take to go to hell? . . . Nothing . . . it's like a default setting on your computer. It's as if most people have allowed their lives to be on autopilot for a collision course with a lake of fire.[3] Repeatedly, the Bible clearly reveals this to be true.

How then does a person plan and prepare to go to Heaven? Where is the road that leads to God? To some, the answer might seem offensive. To many, it seems narrow minded and at the very least, politically incorrect. Jesus said, "I am the way . . ." *(emphatically)* no one, "no one comes to the Father except through me."[4]

You see, where a person spends eternity really boils down to what they believe about Jesus Christ. C.S. Lewis, the renowned author of *The Chronicles of Narnia*, which includes *The Lion, the Witch and the Wardrobe*, is one of history's greatest human minds. He wrote in *Mere Christianity*, and I quote:

> A man who was merely a man and said the sort of things Jesus said would not be a great moral teacher. He would either be a lunatic–on a level with the man who says he is a poached egg–or else he would be the Devil of Hell. You must make your choice. Either this man was, and is, the Son of God: or else a madman or something worse. You can shut Him up for a fool, you can spit at Him and kill Him as a demon; or you can fall at His feet and call Him Lord and God. But let us not come with any patronizing nonsense about His being a great human teacher. He has not left that open to us.[5]

(Music begins)

Jesus said, there is only one way to Heaven . . . and He longs and desires for every person to come live with Him in paradise.

Only One Way

(Narration begins after Only One Way *ends)*

WORSHIP LEADER: The price for us to get to Heaven has been paid in full by Jesus, Himself. Every person who will reach out with their whole heart and believe that He is the only way . . . that He died for their sins . . . anyone who will, in child-like faith, trust Jesus and follow Him, will one day be taken to the place where He lives . . . Heaven.

For those of us who are followers of Christ, there is a calm assurance that we are bound for "the promised land." Is there something that wells up inside you . . . something that gives you a confidence that you are Heaven bound? Can you remember the time when you personally asked Jesus Christ to come into your life and be your Savior? I pray that every person who hears my voice, knows for certain they are going to Heaven one day.

How often do any of us seriously think about Heaven? The early Christians had a "preoccupation" with it.[6] "Until recently the doctrine of Heaven was enormously important" to the saints of God.[7] Today, we hear very little teaching or preaching about the place called Heaven.

What do we know about it? First, Heaven is a city, where God resides . . . where there are buildings, culture, events, people engaged in activity, gatherings and conversations.[8] Heaven is described as a "country" . . . where there is territory and citizens.[9] The Old Testament patriarch, Abraham ". . . looked for a city which hath foundations, whose builder and maker is God.[10] Abraham's descendants were ". . . longing for a better country– a heavenly one . . ."[11] where "God hath prepared for them a City."[12] We, the followers of Jesus, are like pilgrims and strangers, *(music begins)* ". . . looking for the city that is to come."[13]

View the City

Soon We Will See

(Narration begins after Soon We Will See *ends)*

WORSHIP LEADER: The end of our present world is nearer than we think. Soon we will see the portals of Glory. It is beyond words to describe. Yes, we will have eyes to see and ears to hear . . . Jesus said He was going back to Heaven to prepare a place for us . . . and that soon we will see Him . . . Jesus, The Lamb.

Jesus is called "the Lamb" 27 times in Revelation, the last book of the Bible. You see, Heaven is centered around Jesus, the Lamb. Once we arrive, all of our attention will be focused on Him. He is what makes Heaven, Heaven . . . for He is the one who made it possible for each of us to be there.

Take a journey to Heaven with me for a moment. I want to fast forward all of us to Glory. The rapture has taken place; the dead in Christ have all risen from their graves . . . our loved ones who have gone before us are standing right beside us . . . let me read you a scene that God has recorded for us in the book of Revelation:

"And I beheld, and, lo, in the midst of the throne and of the four beasts, and in the midst of the elders, stood a Lamb as it had been slain"[14] . . . and when he had taken the book, the four beasts and four and twenty elders fell down before the Lamb,"[15] "having every one of them harps, and golden bowls of incense, which are the prayers of saints."[16] "And they sung a new song, saying, Thou art worthy to take the book, and to open the seals thereof: for thou was slain, and hast redeemed us to God by thy blood out of every kindred, and tongue, and people, and nation;"[17]

"And I beheld, and I heard the voice of many angels round about the throne and the beasts and the elders: and the number of them was ten thousand times ten thousand, and thousands of thousands; Saying with a loud voice, Worthy is the Lamb that was slain to receive power, and riches, and wisdom, and strength, and honor, and glory, and blessing.[18] ". . . and, lo, a great multitude, which no man could number, of all nations, and kindreds, and people, and tongues, stood before the throne, and before the Lamb, clothed with white robes, and palms in their hands;"[19] (That's you and me!) "And cried with a loud voice, saying, Salvation to our God which sitteth upon the throne, and unto the Lamb. And all the angels stood round about the throne, and about the elders and the four beasts, and fell before the throne on their faces, *(music begins)* and worshipped God."[20]

Worship at the Throne

(Following Worship at the Throne, *Mike recommends singing with the congregation. The Worship Leader could sing the third verse of* Jesus Paid It All *in D-flat or E-flat, ["When before the throne . . ."] which would allow the congregation to join on the chorus. Mike would then suggest leading the congregation in singing the third verse of* Amazing Grace *in F ["When we've been there . . ."]. This would work best by utilizing words on a screen,*

but could also be printed in a program. Another option could be I Can Only Imagine, What a Day That Will Be *[chorus] or some other appropriate song for the moment.)*

(Narration begins after Worship at the Throne *ends)*

Worship Leader: There will be no personal music preferences or music styles in Heaven. We'll finally worship as one . . . and we will worship perfectly. The sound of praise will fill the heavens . . . and there will be no theological debates or denominational divisions.

You know, there are many Christians who have never heard a message on Heaven. Satan is busy keeping God's children from setting their hearts and minds on things above. He knows that when we are "Heavenly minded," we become more like Jesus . . . we become better servants of the Lord. The enemy will do everything he can to keep us from becoming more like Christ.

As I have studied about Heaven, I have become a better Christian. By looking at what God is preparing for us, I have become more aware of God's love for us. It has inspired me to live more holy and to strive to be more pleasing to the Lord. I am also more keenly aware of how the material things in this world . . . are only temporary.

For just a moment, would you allow your mind to dream . . . and imagine what Heaven will be like? Try to picture what your new home might look like. We know that when we take our last breath, we will be absent from this earthly body and instantly present with the Lord. For a little while, we will be in Heaven with a temporary form, waiting for the resurrection and the rapture of the saints.

Eventually, we will live in a glorified body in a glorified world. Yes, we will have brand new bodies, fashioned after the resurrected body of Jesus . . . and we will know one another. Every reference in the book of Revelation reveals that we will also have our five senses. I used to think that we would not have memory in Heaven. However, there is scriptural evidence that we will have memory, but that it will be free of pain or sorrow.

If you depart for Heaven before the rapture of the church, I believe you will have an ability to know what is happening on earth. If this were not true, how could there be ". . . rejoicing in the presence of the angels of God over one sinner who repents."[21] In Revelation 19, we read that the inhabitants of Heaven begin rejoicing and shouting "Hallelujah," and praising God for specific events that are happening on earth.[22]

Because of the coming resurrection, we will be able to physically embrace one another once again. We think of Heaven as "less real and less substantial" than this present existence but it is more real and more substantial, because it is eternal . . . we won't be ghosts or "shadow people" . . . we will have bodies that are recognizable . . . we will be "fully alive and fully physical in a fully physical universe."[23]

Jesus died that we might have a "resurrected life on a resurrected earth."[24] The children of God, those that follow Jesus, have a longing in their heart to go to Heaven. It is where we belong . . . in the land where we'll never grow old. And Heaven will *feel* like home! Each of us will have our own place . . . Jesus went to prepare it for us . . . "a place where we fit right in"[25] . . . everything will be perfect for us. Jesus is the carpenter from Nazareth that "knows how to build."[26]

Did you know that God is going to relocate the New Jerusalem to the New Earth? The apostle John saw a city, which was in Heaven, coming down to earth. We are going to live on the New Earth and God will live with us and among us. Few of us ever think about God's dwelling place, one day being on the earth.

At 86 years old, while banished to a small Island called Patmos, the apostle John caught a glimpse of that Heavenly land:

"And I saw a new heaven and a new earth: for the first heaven and the first earth were passed away; and there was no more sea. And I John saw the holy city, new Jerusalem, coming down from God out of heaven, prepared as a bride adorned for her husband. And I heard a great voice out of heaven saying, Behold, the tabernacle of God is with men, and he will dwell with them, and they shall be his people, and God himself shall be with them, and be their God. And God shall wipe away all tears from their eyes; and there shall be no more death, neither sorrow, nor crying, neither shall there be any more pain: for the former things are passed away.

And I saw no temple therein: for the Lord God Almighty and the Lamb are the temple of it. And the city had no need of the sun, neither of the moon, to shine in it: for the glory of God did lighten it, and the Lamb is the light thereof. And the gates of it shall not be shut at all by day: for there shall be no night there. And there shall in no wise enter into it any thing that defileth, neither whatsoever worketh abomination, or maketh a lie: but they which are written in the Lamb's book of life."[27]

I don't know about you, but I am excited about my eternal home. I have a great anticipation of seeing loved ones again and talking with Abraham, Moses, and Elijah . . . but my greatest longing is to see the One who died for me.

"What a day, glorious day that will be!"[28]

The First Day of Forever

NOTES

1. Randy Alcorn, *Heaven* (Carol Stream: Tyndale House Publishers, Inc., 2004), xix.
2. Randy Alcorn, *Heaven*, 33.
3. Randy Alcorn, *Heaven*, 23.
4. John 14:6, NIV
5. C. S. Lewis, *Mere Christianity* (San Francisco: HarperCollins Publishers), 52.
6. Randy Alcorn, *Heaven*, xvii.
7. Randy Alcorn, *Heaven*, 9.
8. Randy Alcorn, *Heaven*, 78.
9. Randy Alcorn, *Heaven*, 78.
10. Hebrews 11:10, KJV
11. Hebrews 11:16, NIV
12. Hebrews 11:16, 21st Century KJV
13. Hebrews 13:14, NIV
14. Revelation 5:6, KJV
15. Revelation 5:8, KJV
16. Revelation 5:8, NIV
17. Revelation 5:9; KJV
18. Revelation 5:11-12, KJV
19. Revelation 7:9, KJV
20. Revelation 7:10-11; KJV
21. Luke 15:10, NIV
22. Revelation 19:1-2, NIV
23. Randy Alcorn, *Heaven*, 137.
24. Randy Alcorn, *Heaven*, 137.
25. Randy Alcorn, *Heaven*, 163.
26. Randy Alcorn, *Heaven*, 164.
27. Revelation 21:1-4, 22-23, 25, 27, KJV
28. *What a Day That Will Be*